MW00677528

THE WISHING TOMB

Also by Amanda Auchter

The Glass Crib, 2011
Light Under Skin, 2006 (chapbook)

THE WISHING TOMB

AMANDA AUCHTER

PERUGIA PRESS
FLORENCE, MASSACHUSETTS
2012

Copyright © 2012 by Amanda Auchter

All rights reserved

Perugia Press extends deeply felt thanks to the many individuals whose generosity made the publication of *The Wishing Tomb* possible. Perugia Press is a tax-exempt, nonprofit 501(c)(3) corporation publishing first and second books of poetry by women. To make a tax-deductible donation, please contact us directly or visit our Web site.

Book Design by Susan Kan, Jeff Potter, and Amanda Auchter.

Cover art and author photograph by Eddy Roberts (see eddyroberts.com).

Library of Congress Cataloging-in-Publication Data

Auchter, Amanda.

  The wishing tomb / Amanda Auchter.

    p. cm.

  ISBN 978-0-9794582-5-5

  1. New Orleans (La.)--Poetry. I. Title.

  PS3601.U337W57 2012

  811'.6--dc23

                          2012012001

Perugia Press

P.O. Box 60364

Florence, MA 01062

info@perugiapress.com

http://www.perugiapress.com

CONTENTS

III.

THE WISHING TOMB

The city, however, does not tell its past,
but contains it like the lines of a hand.
—Italo Calvino

I.

LETTER TO COMTE DE PONTCHARTRAIN

December, 1697

The question is water, how to shadow

this slow tongue that collects

in hill and dale, wild cattle. To build
a city made of birds, cotton, rain-

                lit houses. How to harvest
and fell

white mulberry, copper, the buffalo
air. Imagine a country risen

from ship timber, Indian corn. The windows

and their hemp sashes. Here,

it is easy to remain still and sweat
at midnight, your body a seething

              sea. Everywhere
it is dark: loose leaves,

forest. The water
arrives exhausted, climbs

the lowlands and marshweed. We will want

to close its wide mouth, bring boats

              stacked with cables, ropes,
masts. We could conjure

a city from fruit blossom, magnolia,
thunderheads. This world is in me:

let us build ourselves again

                    from silt, salt. Let the water
rise and wash

through the streets. Let the wind
fill each breath, each dry throat.

EARLY PASTORAL

New Orleans, 1718

We are approaching the marshweed and sycamore, the gnarled low trees and cypress. For weeks the boat has rocked us, a nauseous lullaby. The days have slipped through our bodies with the sound of sea swells, the rain and its humid talk. The land opens before us: the first point of green. Here is the beginning of a house: lumber ships untether their long pale beams. Here is the mouth of the river, its arterial flow. We are approaching the lowlands, the docks. We watch the shoreline near: a man waves his arms in the air. For weeks we have imagined what we will come to, what land will claim us. For weeks, we have talked of gold streets and haystacks, pockets heavy with coins. We never imagined so much water, the stench of bodies led away in chains. The mosquito-darkened sky. We watch the town open and open. The first glint of light, smoke. Soon we are standing on the shore and the heat stuns us. We watch a man lead away another man by his shackled neck until we cannot see him. So many bodies. A woman stands in the coal dusk, waving goodbye. Her skin soot-bright in the dark rising tide. How much we wanted this: the sky's blue bowl, our lives stripped clean. White oak. Magnolia bark. The docked ship.

CASKET GIRLS

—our stockings and silk
garters for you, a hand
to hold to your mouth, a hand

to breathe into, to collect
the blossom of a wrist. We long
to long, to bend our limbs—

We thought the water would never
end. Dark pools of stars
in our faces—

We thought until we wore
out thinking, until the ocean
ended, and we

ended at shoreline, an anchor
dropped. A casket
burst open. The ghost-

body of a dress, a pair of gloves
floated beneath us, then sank—

THE GOOD FRIDAY FIRE
1788

Iron-charred, the embers blurred the daylight
sky into smoke, curtains on fire. We searched

through the ashes for the city, its bowl of paper

crushed and wrought. The axe-hewn cypress
shingles, the bedposts and thumbed Bibles. Each
wide and shallow-hipped roof, peels of paint

from Chartres Street to Dauphine, from St. Philip
(saint of the cooks and bakers elbow-deep in flour

and ovens) to Conti to Toulouse, everything
a charred wick.

        Before there was the storm
of white ash, the syllables of burst windows

and collapsed beams, the streets a wilderness
of ruins. Before the impossible language
of soot drifts, of children's eyes

burned colorless, there was a lighted candle
on the altar of a home chapel,

a man on his knees, prayer burning

in his mouth. The tongues of fire ignited
behind him, carved arcs in the afternoon

wind. The bright explosion of heat, hymn.

THE PUNISHMENT COLLAR

In the white noise of winter, a collar
of bells sound the location

of a man throwing his shadow

through live oaks, cotton bramble. The strange
storm of heartbeat, damp

adrenaline. Behind him, the house falls
into mist and branches,

                    an oil-glow behind a curtain.

His body a leaf turned over
and over. The low brushwood

and stones. In the distance:
gun shots, horse hooves. The seconds

           piled between. His body
just entering air, a bird tangled in stone sky.

The sharp grass. The real blades
             and their scars, their unstitched mouths.

The light that once caught his white-
              bloomed sclera. The hand that came

down, the open palm, the broken tooth. There
were plantains everywhere. The music

exploded in his ear. Tonight, he is the wind

but not the light. Not the fields swept
and cleared, the barbed neck.

Not the hands that worked

               the cane and clover.

CHLOE

What I remember—the white
pitcher on the coffee table offered

    steam. Mr. Woodruff's fingers, a spool

of silk that thumbed my throat. The clock
that chimed four times. The sound

of the children's footsteps
on the stairs. And then this—

           out in the barn, where

one crow perched on the high beams,
a thread of straw in its dark mouth. My face

in his hands. My face in the blade, the blood,
the dirt. I want to believe that

        as he opened the large door,

he could not look back at me, the way I held
my hand to my head, the newly ragged flesh until

    everything became dark and quiet. I remember

his boots beside me. A rag tossed down
like a small grief. And this—

        a woman opening her mouth,

the pale smear of oleander sugar on her lips. And the girls
that came into the room too early, dipped

their fingers into the frosting, licked the sweetness
again and again. I could not stop them. I watched

the hearthsmoke rise, the girls and their cake.
I turned to the window.

      The branches of a low tree scraped the ground.

OUR LADY OF PROMPT
SUCCOR SPEAKS OF FIRE

What had I imagined at the open window: the ash
     of passion vine, thistle, white clover? The dark

sash lifted: houses there, then gone. The sky,
     its unresisting blue above the bowl of smoke. The light

opened onto my face. The light, its haywire
     through shingles and leaves. I held the singed oaks,

edible flowers to my face in the squares of glass.
     What was I supposed to do? I was not the light,

the heartbeat there in that small pane of sparks. I touched
     the wind. The air hummed with burning. The air

crowded the garden, the window with its cluster of sparks. I asked
     of the light to spare the bird in the thin limb of a mimosa.

The light continued its silent wreckage. I was given to
     the orange coins of flames to collect its breath in my chest.

To keep the door on the hinge, the ceiling unscathed. The room
     filled with kneeling, with skirts sweeping the floor.

The wind changed direction, turned the fire away. I pressed
     into its gold smoke, a thread passing through.

REPORT ON LEVEE BREACH, 1816

We press ourselves into the shredded seams,
    sandbag the breach. The large sun burns

overhead, while a white man whips mules
with a chicory whip. And our backs:

    sweat-shined, marked. At night,

we keep vigil, listen to the water
        suck in debris and spit it out

again. We do not speak of how soon the water
will reach the porch, the window, the roof.

    We do not speak at all,

but watch the man in the cart shout orders
        in the distance, how his mule shakes off

mosquitoes, dust. Salt pools our collarbones,
stings our eyes. We are of the water, its moon-

shards, the desperate way it breaks through
        whatever contains it: sediment,

brushwood, tall grass. And how too we are this
broken joint in the earth, its cracked jaw,

    a tooth spat out and lost.

TESTIMONY OF BARONESS DE PONTALBA, 1834

How animal I am in my desire
to live: my body a plague

                of gunshots, starburst
wounds. My body brooding in the damp

                heat of breath, of the pistol-
echo in my ears. My fingers a broken nest

wrapped in sinew, bone. I listen to the red drum

of my heart, its blood a wind

carrying through me. I held my fingers up
to my chest, a motion of *no*

or *stop*. Each bullet collapsed
                inside me, the red silking

through my clothes, the afternoon. How spectacular
                the pain: a fire burning

through a dry field. A house undone. How alive
I am here in the winter light,

                in the silver thread
of smoke. I held up my hands,

turned away.
                My voice swung back into my throat.

HARRIET BEECHER STOWE AT THE CORNSTALK HOTEL, 1850

A man and a woman arrive together

in chains. His voice surfaces—
I shall try to meet you there—but I cannot

hear what follows. Tea cools in white china.
I think of horses, the way they walk back

and forth, hold up their heads. Horses,
the way a man in a coat turns them about,

      opens their mouths, checks their teeth. Scars

on the flanks. A chimney gasps smoke
into the afternoon. The body looted. A child

plays a violin outside the stalls, watches
as women remove their handkerchiefs,

          show their hands. A whip

weaves close to the ears. The balcony overlooks
a narrow street, a cart and driver.

      The voices drift out, an edge

of an outline. The voices say, *I hope
you will try to meet me in heaven.*

        I shall try to meet you there.

AMERICAN PLAGUE

I. Early Stage

Everywhere, water, night pushing
its mouth into the humid,

sleeping bodies. Mosquitoes

in the ears, eyelids, bleed
from the heartpulse

of the neck. This is a city
in ruins, a bridge of ache,

nausea, jaundice. Houses filled

with netting, windows drawn
to keep out the dark

silence, the hot rhythm

of insects touching the glass,
the first child who walked

through the door, bright fingernail
scratches on her arms,

face. Her fever. Her flush.

II. Period of Remission

In the house, a man brings a bowl
to the table. The children watch

the bowl fill with water, watch a jar
empty of leeches, how each one unfurls

like a rotten tongue. In the bowl,
four tongues suspended,

unanswerable. Each girl

hooks to them, their skin a raspberry
bruise, ingested. Sunburn,

rope-sting, switch-whip. Tongues

and the subtle suck of fine hair
and flesh. In the bowl,

a mosquito dabs the water, glances rim,
table, wooden spoon, pale scalp.

For a while, the children taste rain, wild-
flower, sugared bread. For a while,

there is no fever, no fire beneath the skin.

III. Period of Intoxication

Come holy, the hands anointing
the collapsed star of the face,

tongue. A house

filled with candles, frozen
breath. Soon, delirium,

the fevered sight. The body

lit to ash, suffering. The body
a flamed branch,

dead field. Come

hemorrhage, seizure, fingers
bird-wild, violet. Come, assemble

the last flight, the sun's quiet

compass. The mosquito
that brushes eyelid, collarbone,

bruises the blood. The fever

made of tender wings, water,
dusk. Come, lay down in sleep,

the body's bright tulip flush.

THE DISORDERED BODY

Rain falls from the black skies daily, the city

a shroud of rot: garbage and heat and humidity,
the bright stink

of bodies. The body a branch after lightning, a language

of fever, delirium. At the riverfront, our children
watch boats come

and go, scratch their dark arms until they bleed. What language
must we speak to keep safe?
Every prayer a tongue of fire, every psalm

a child's cry deep into the night. A child who unfolds

her body into dark sweat, damp hair. We are drowning
in this mosquito dusk, our bodies

inside a sea of stings. We are emptying our pails

and wash buckets and still they settle into hairlines,
fingertips. We have long practiced

disaster. We do not hide in our beds and closets,
close a door, a mouth. We do not
say it will not come. It will come.

It will bring its terrible song, hum it into our houses.

MOURNING BROOCH AND EARRINGS, c. 1866

How strange the body's harvest: knots
of hair threaded into brooch, earrings, gold
hair clipped after the last exhale, after

the drained sun closes

over the eyes, the mouth, the bare
autumn trees. Consider how much grief

in the cutting, the collecting, the silence

of sewing tendril, sideburn, wisp
of bangs. How no one will wear this,

pin the coiled hair onto collar
or coat, will hook the small
braids to earlobes. In a room,

someone hums and threads, hums

and threads. The hair clings
to thimble, rug. Faint webs of it
drift through the dark air,

breathe, land, breathe.

SISTER XAVIER'S HERB GARDEN

For sprain, bring bay leaf. For rheumatism,
oregano. Let fever become

                lavender blossom, summer
savory, aromatic in the late afternoon. For insomnia,

                dillweed. Let the sunlight petal
the garden, heal the ulcerative stomachs

and mouths. For digestion, yarrow; anxiety, skullcap.

Each a bundle to strip and rinse, crush into a tea.

Let buds burst forth—sage, caraway, anise—
Let the damp cough become marigold;

the fluttered heart, pennyroyal. Everything
                transformed: the blood a field.

The blood blooms into ginger, lemon balm. And the woman
                fills her baskets. And the woman

looks up from her language: chamomile,

                hawthorn, the sweet mint in her hands.

MARIE LAVEAU

St. John's Eve

As night pushes its mouth through
the bayou, I float wreaths of milk-

weed, dragonhead, evening primrose
down the river. On the weedy banks,

a wreath becomes a body,

submerged. Tangle of yellow
bundles of hair, a corpus of sticks

and buds, its weight lowering
into the deep. For weeks,

to keep evil away, I filled rooms

with dried blooms, this wild-
flower decay. Its scent slipped through

windows, framed the face of my weeping

icons. Tonight, I throw ox-eye,
dotted mint into the current, build

a shoreline of fire and blossom,

leap the embers. O Saint John, water
fills me. Release my tongue

into the charred sky. My tongue,
a wilderness, a voice being born.

LOVE SPELL WITH HAIR AND OIL

In every room, I give my hands
busy work: water

poured into a vase, fasten pearl buttons
on Miss J.'s dress. I touch her hair, whisper:
your husband comes home with another woman's talc.

This I can cure. I understand how a man carries
sex home with him as though it were a bag
of onions, knotted with twine and already rotting

in his fingers. Miss J. husks corn for dinner,
watches as I burn sage

throughout the house, how my body reflects

back in the great windows. My body a gnarled oak,
iron gate, gas lamp. After I fill the house

with the green earth smoke, I splash her neck
with sandalwood oil, tell her of its fragrant
wood, its fine-grain magic. To do this

each night: dab between breasts, thighs, jut

of collarbone, to keep him in her bed. On
the full moon, I say, when the light rises
through the oaks, when the street disappears

into silver, light a red candle, crush roses

into your skin, let your breath
touch his mouth, wrist. The bright

heat of your bodies, the small tides.

MARIE LAVEAU, POSTMORTEM

Look—I am devil's shoestring, crushed

mandrake root. A bag left on a doorstep
filled with white clover, shark's tooth,

dove's blood. From where I am, I listen
to the rum-mouths, a window

opening onto Canal Street, the sound

of a hand tossing damp earth back
into the ground. I am the story that gets told,

the crow on the iron gate. The burn
of guinea peppers under the tongue,
the straight pin through the small cloth

heart. Violent moon, the grass wreath burning

in the bayou, the scatter of white oak bark
along the dark river. Let me stay

among the baskets filled with coins
and cigars, the letters written on my grave
in red brick dust. To see again

the hands that last held my hair,
my neck, the blade. For the wind

to blow through me. A garden to weed.

DECORATING THE TOMBS: ALL SAINTS' DAY

After the wood engraving by John Durkin, November 1885

We bring our bread and fall flowers,

a table spread with rust linen,
forks and plates. We bring paper crowns,

a sheaf of wheat, press each against white-
washed tombs, offer our prayers, our baskets
of harvest: yellow chrysanthemums,

red coxcombs, wreaths of black glass
beads. Keepsakes in the glow

of our children's hands, fields
of candlelight, lamp oil, the distant

burst of lightning. Each stone
a vessel we bring our mouths to, touch
and whisper, wipe clear of lichen, soot.

Around us, the city blurs in dusk: low blue

between the coliseum of houses, men
with their carts of ice, tomatoes. We lift

our spoons of pudding and don't speak
of the rising river, fevers, how soon the damp
earth will shutter our eyes, dredge the backs

of our throats. How soon, too, the night
will come, the rats for our crumbs,

the water, the ruin, for our tender bones.

II.

A BRIEF HISTORY WITH DOCUMENTS

Tourgée to Plessy

They will want to take you into the field, fill you
with bullets. They have been known

to make a man disappear. They will call you
coon and *boy*. They will yell *pull him off*

while showing you their revolvers, their lips
spit-slick, white. No one will look up

from their newspapers or from the window
where a crow dives from a tree. No one will see

the way you keep silent, decorous. They will
expect a fight. They will expect

trouble, blood, a scene. Do not pretend
you are anything but what you are: a man

just passing through. A man
who kissed his wife at the door,

who sits in the best car while the sun
warms his face. A man sipping coffee,

turning his ticket over and over in his hands.

ORDER OF THE GARTER

In this carpeted ballroom, I answer
to *Camellia*, *Violet*, wild-

flowers on the tip of the tongue. Each name

a promise of sweetness, dark
honey. I've learned the look well,
the danger of it: how men imagine

my body underneath garters and dresses,
high-heeled boots. My hands,

darker than any one of their faces. Music

drifts through an open window and I drink
the wine I am offered, spin its scarlet thread

in the clear glass. Each gaze freezes me

in place: my jut of collarbone, small
brooch at my throat. I pretend

I am stone, wood, something difficult

to break. When I am led up the staircase,
I let him touch my wrist, tell me
a joke. I do not look at him, but instead

listen to his breathing, its damp weight

against my mouth. For a while, I leave

my body, watch the dusklight

shadow the window sashes, the cockroach
climbing the wallpaper. The fractured shapes

of my body in the broken vanity mirror.

PHOTOGRAPH OF HILMA BURT'S MIRRORED BALLROOM WITH JELLY ROLL MORTON, 1907

Eight women practice the music
of their bodies: white dresses

raised to show ankles, a suggestion

of pale calves, stockings. Behind them,
the mirrored wall repeats their gardenia-

blossomed hair, the way they lean
their hips into the piano player,

touch him with their floral-sweat

scent. He is young, background,
an ear, a coat, a few fingers floating

above the keys. The mirror too high

to hold anything but an idea of dark
hair, eyebrows, forehead. Each sound

he names, the sharps and flats, each
a woman dancing, a woman

turning toward the camera, her voice

a scale repeating itself into the flash-
bright walls, the gesture of his fingers

lifted before the first sound comes out.

MAYANN

Fat-fingered, you clutch the dark
ring of my breast while the Gulf sheds
its August steam into the streets. For a while

I kept you in the drawer next to my slips
and stockings. For a while, I stood

at the doorway, skirt lifted

to show smooth calf, ankle, knee
while you slept, your lips sucking in the red-
lighted air of Perdido Street. What life

I give you: the music of streetcars,
hailstones, sex. The unfamiliar

voices of men: chair-scrape, the drum

of belt buckles hitting the floor. Dear
son, do not remember me holding hats,
trousers, my legs open

to the cracked ceiling. Instead, think
of my magnolia hair, the blossom
of my body on your tongue. Years from now,

empty your lungful of notes

into the bird-blackened streets. Somewhere
in a leaf-thickened courtyard,

I will be rubbing a man out of my clothes,
and listening to you, your trumpet

mouth filled with my name, this shotgun
stoop, echoing the river-licked sky.

WASHER WOMAN, 1917

In the imagined photograph
of my great-grandmother Rosselli, she holds

a tub of a rich woman's clothes—the silks
                    and blood-darkened rags—

as she must have in those days
under the Louisiana sun, as so many

like her—immigrant-tongued, olive-skinned—

held out buckets of wash for a camera or for
the sister with them to take inside for ironing.

In this photograph, she is like the water
                    that darkens with a week's worth

of dirt and sweat. The water falling from her
red-scraped knuckles

                    back into the tin bucket, splashing

the grass. Soon, she will return to kneel
into a family's linens and buttons, the washboard,

the morning light that burns its pale reed
                    into her face. Soon, she will

carry home her aches and sour perfume—
carbolic soap, powdered soda,

a pot of red beans cooking on a stove.

THE GOOD FRIDAY FLOOD, 1927

The sky tongues its way into houses,

into hot water cornbread rising
out of the pan. Someone sings *trouble*

the water, adds flour to roux, parboils
rice. Rosary-fisted, someone kneels

to the floor, says, *swallow me back,*

Oh Lord. Death, a box packed
with photographs, quilts, trumpets,

song. Here, the river erases each street's face,
buries houses where they stand:

street-scattered, drowned. Each window
bursts, cowrie shells thrown into the dark

floodwater. Tonight, it wants bodies,

will catch a man who looks
for a dropped cigarette, brand him

with briars, mud, the bones of dead birds,
before raising him against a splintered fence,

tree limbs, a car upended in the yard.

TESTIMONY OF EVANGELINE
THE OYSTER GIRL, 1948

I'm the river city attraction. My hair the color of sea-

weed, rotten marsh. My body slips nightly
from the pink mouth of the oyster shell, slips

into the white lights, into pockets of coins and bills,
a glass sweating on a dark table. Understand that

when the girl came out with her fish tank act,
her nude swimming, goldfish clinging to her hair,

I saw my name dim from the headline, from
the rounds of Sazeracs, the cocktail cherries,

small straws like hard little tongues. I saw myself
back in the cotton fields of my childhood, mosquito-

stung, a basket under my arm. I saw the hatchet
in my fist, the burst tank. The water, the girl, the fish.

How each broken shard was a glittered jewel, an applause.

DO YOU KNOW WHAT IT MEANS

Satchmo, you returned to this paddleboat
city as King of Zulu, king

        of blackface and grass skirts,
jazzed tongue blowing into the confetti

        of beads. Louis, you returned
to your Storyville streets, the red lights

long gone out. You returned to the ghost

of your mother, her peignoir past noon, her body
a book flipped open. Here is your childhood,

the wheelbarrow, the coal you drug into dusk
        before you could read, before

you could blow. Satchel Mouth,
you waved your hand into the swamp

        of memory, looked through
a window at ice clinking in glasses

you were not allowed to touch. You turned away,
boarded a plane, watched the city

        grow distant. Dark

    as a mouth with its teeth removed. The city,
a song you wrote at 30,000 feet.

THE HEEL STRING GANG

One called his slash *shackles*

and switch whips. Another, *a body bruised*
and starved. Each considered the blade,

the broken spring of tendon, flesh. The heel

string that kept their feet walking
through high grass, briars, the low bramble
of cotton plants. Each man torn and hot

under the Louisiana sun, each one
with a woman's name under

his tongue like a whittled blade

kept under a flat pillow. Out in the fields,
the men gathered around an oak tree,

watched the razor edge through dark

skin, the ligaments snap like the bright pop
of the warden's fist against jawbones. The fire-

burn of soft tissue, the sharp-bladed scream.

THE ANGOLA INMATE
COFFIN FACTORY

Another afternoon of sweat and nails and
someone's thumb busted and split,

stripped like the pine box cleaned
of knotholes, bark, beetles. The dark

flesh, a howl. Watch the clock
the guards, the clock. Listen

to the cacophony of hammers beating
boards into coffins. The floor covered

in sawdust, its pale ash. Each man
who dies hopes someone will come for him,

collect his body, his small relics: thumbed
magazines, a Bible, water-stained letters. His hands

shake. He holds the nail or else he strikes
it once, twice. He hopes for his body

to get out of here, for his mouth
to open to earth, his sister's tears. He dreams

of hammers, a field. Of his body
splintered, unclaimed. His body buried

in ragged weeds, tall grass. His hands
striking lumber. His fist rising, falling.

THE EDUCATION OF
RUBY BRIDGES, 1960

Child, do not suffer the guns drawn
                    near your face, or the voices

that pass through open windows, through
the prick of the tongues that own them. Child,

this is no place for tears. Close your eyes

against the crush of pickets and bullhorns,
                    the language of bricks

wrapped in cloth and flung from car windows,
of the Black doll in a coffin tossed at your feet

as you climb the steps. The lesson flickers gray
                    and white throughout the country, stains

palms on each doorstep. In this city, the syllables
drag like a rope, scatter on sidewalks and grass.

                    Remember who you are

in this story. You are the meaning, Child.

A book spread open. A flutter in the sky.

BILLION-DOLLAR BETSY

September 9, 1965

During those days, I coughed cars, telephone
lines, kicked down doors. Inside, a mother

> and two children in a hallway closet
> watched as I sucked everything

into my wide throat—coffee tables, lamps, pictures
of babies and grandmothers. It was like slipping

> a dress over my head, so easy and thoughtless,
> the way I lifted up through the rafters and beams,

let the sky pour down, let the river spine inside
sills and wooden frames. I was a woman glowing

> in the dark, fluorescent and visible, a spool
> on a radar, my voice a train in the ear. I was

a woman with only a day's worth of hours
to collect trees, shatter glass, burst

> the city's earthen seams. I listened to my heart
> drum over the rooftops and levees: my heart

a fluttered red thing. An oil fire
in the middle of the road. A scrap

> of aluminum slicing a branch. A swamp rose
> twisting under the darkest sky.

HIGHWAY PASTORAL

For months we watched oak trees disappear
from the esplanade on North Claiborne Avenue

on the backs of trucks. Men in hard hats

walked past LaBranche's Drug Store
                              and The Capital Theater
as we continued to barbeque from Canal Street

down to St. Bernard. We tended our azaleas,
                    wiped clean kitchens and lunch counters.
It was slow how it unraveled: first the trees, then

the flowers. Gone. The men
                    walked up and down the road

with clipboards. We watched from the windows
of People's Life Insurance the larger trucks move in

with their bellies of concrete. At night,
the children stamped their hands and feet

                              into the white softness, drug their fingers
into the shapes of their names. At Charbonnet Funeral Home,
                    Armand sewed the mouths of the dead. We dreamed

of jackhammers, clouds of dust. We wore the dust
                    to work at Two Sisters and Gilbert's Toy Store,
then saw the shops close, the gardens ribbon into concrete.

The men came with their slick mouths, gestured into cameras.

The trucks brought their stink and steel. The sun
slivered overhead while the men brought their shovels

and drank tea from thermoses. We sat into the dusk,
                              watched our silhouettes
of lawn chairs and cigarettes braid the ground.

POPE JOHN PAUL II VISITS
NEW ORLEANS, 1987

In a lakefront field, a woman lifts her hands
              to the thunderheads blooming
        above, to the silver coins

of raindrops just beginning to fall. She can feel
              the heat of bodies
        offering up their missing limbs,

their drug-addicted sons, their stillborn. Her
              prayers hang inside her throat,
        the words for God lost in afternoon

sweat, noise. When she sees him take the stage,
              she whispers *tumors, bone grafts, lungs*
        filled with ash. A thousand yellow flowers. A bare cross

overlooking the wind-stirred grass. She gives herself
              to the wind, to his voice caught in updraft,
        to the water he sprinkles into air. She crosses herself

as it touches forehead, sunburned shoulders. She wants it
              to sting, to prove itself on her skin. To find
        a way inside the miracle of a voice suspended

in a stone sky. For the water, the miracle to collapse
              the dark spores illuminated in X-ray light,
        to arrow into her ribs. To know her name.

THE CHICKEN MAN WALKS
THE QUARTER

Down here, the bone-pale hours keep

the broken down
                broken down:

  a sugar-mouthed girl
on Esplanade with a man in her throat,

a blade in her shoe. At night,
everyone needs something
                          to believe in:

  my *gris-gris*, chicken claw,
snaketooth. I walk the streets:

                Burgundy, Dauphine, Bourbon,

      offer bags of *ju ju* to the junkies
                      with their needle-drawn prayers,

each turn a beautiful, bad road.
On the Neutral Ground, someone

asks about my last show, if I really broke
                  the chicken's neck, drank

                  its blood from the throat. How

  I swallow glass shards, kiss fire

and not burn. I light a cigarette
            in front of his face and we listen

        to the city's blue music of bottles

and trumpets, breathe its chicory-
        sweat, listen

to its desperate magic—gunshot, backfire,
a bottle tapped with a stick, keeping time.

THE STELLA/STANLEY
SHOUTING CONTEST

Each syllable bursts through the blue, the balconies

crowded with women, their forearms
on the iron railing. Each lamppost
and shuttered window listen

to this boy's voice, its thunder, its music

the heart's storm drain. This voice,
this *Stella!* a bird falling in air,
a bright broken bead. How her name

beats fast inside him, empties into roof tiles
and streetcars. He falls to his knees,

his body a necklace of sweat, spit. Her name

rises through the jagged heat of his body,
the cloudbursts in the late light. Each time,

her name hollows him out, a name

made of perfume and humidity. Each time,
he presses it all back into his chest—
the flashbulb flood, the scatter

of black birds on the beer-bottled street.

THE WISHING TOMB

Every night, women come with baskets
of fruit, rosaries, clippings of their own dark

braids. Leave candy, and tomorrow
a flower will appear on the doorstep. Tears,
and no one will break

your heart. A love spell scratched in brick:

three red Xs chalk-marked
over my name. Place your hands

over your eyes and circle the weeds, the half-
filled bottles of rum, the bright
beads. Knock three times against this

whitewashed tomb. Listen

to birds rise from magnolia, a man
decanting a saxophone on Iberville. Everything

becomes possible: a plastic rose blooms
to a diamond ring, broken glass,
a divorce. Do not idle among the candies

and coins, the others tapping out their offering,

but touch your lips to your fingers, your fingers
to each X. Give me what you wish:

bread crumbs, earrings, your high-heeled shoe

and I will show you what you've earned:

a rain-smeared kiss, a letter, or nothing
but nights of teacups, an empty bed.

CREOLE TOMATOES

Carmen Leona Reese, 17, a runaway and presumed prostitute,
was one of the six people murdered in New Orleans during a
52-hour stretch in October, 2007.

Early fall, the red natives turn
       soft with blossom-end rot. Each a small wound
              splitting at the corona. Inside, fruit
worms nest the seeds, fibers. The skin softens.

The girl left her home in Texas
       for New Orleans. She listened
              to the sweep of highway pass, watched
headlights slow, then stop.

In the fields, the tomatoes are placed in boxes
       or baskets. They are all overripe, decaying
              under the sun. One falls from the truck,
rolls off into a ditch. A bird begins its descent.

The bruises were too many to count. Each one
       overlapped the other: scarlet ovals
              around her throat. In the photograph,
her eyes were open. The bruises, black.

The tomatoes drop from the vines each day. The black-
       spotted leaves, heavy curtains hanging
              from the busted fruit. Grasshoppers
devour them within seconds.

So far from home and her body
       a ruined map. The sharp hook
              of a flashlight moved over bare feet,
a runner's calves, breasts, a weed-choked alley.

Bacterial wilt. Fernleafing. Yellow mosaic. The tomatoes
       open to heat, drought, late season. The leaves
              streak brown along the stems. Each leaf
a darkened shoestring. The fruit hard as a bone.

On Mandolin Street, the red flesh of sky broke above her
       nude body, above the gravel, the ants, the stained
              mattress in the garbage can. The star-
shaped wound at her temple, another in her chest.

HOLT CEMETERY

after the photograph by Pompo Bresciani

Lay me down in stone with a few cigars,

peanuts. I am learning to sleep with bottles
of Bacardi Rum, loose change, purple beads

left in a tangle of grass. Lay me down

beneath razor wire and cement blocks,
cigarettes smeared with lipstick. The sky

and its gold doubloon. Here, winter rain drifts
through jawbone, a blue vase filled

with artificial tulips, rosary beads, a note folded
and folded. Lay me down

next to the children and the faces in small
lockets and crosses, damp weeds that shred

and land. Break me open into the skein

of engine backfires that toss the air, the gunshot-
fractured haze. Carve my name in cement,

in the shadow of an iron bench, the magnolia

dusk. Lay me down in bed frames,
wooden headstones, planter boxes.

The sidewalk bursting with grass.

III.

WIND PRAYER

Tell me how to speak to suffering, where
to toss the slivers of a body already broken. For months,

      I have imagined this riotous nature: leaves pulled
from banana trees, the black swelled-tide. Which storm

      do I bless with the frozen cross, which one
do I open the door or window to, offer handfuls

      of my prayers? I am preparing myself for weeping
grasses, a future that collects a city. Of drinking

      instant coffee from Styrofoam, emergency
candles. I empty the bag of this ruin

      on the counter next to the mail and apples,
hold each piece to the afternoon

      light. I wait for the sky to burst
into flame or downpour. How bound I am

      by the water, with the memory or fear
of a roof peeled back, the plastic xylophone chime

      of a garbage can twisting down the street.
A hand feeding slivers of bread into the swarm.

ST. LOUIS CATHEDRAL, 2005

The marble Jesus opens his eyes to the violence
　　　　　of wind shaking bananas from tender stems,
　　　　the crack of two oak trees falling

in St. Anthony's Garden behind their ornamental gate.
　　　　　Rivers fill his mouth and in each
　　　　he tastes a shipwreck: torn boards, canvas,

drowned bodies. The slap of purple beads
　　　　　against his bare feet. His arms
　　　　spread out as though he could cradle the city

inside him, as though the water that rises
　　　　　above porches and windowsills,
　　　　above attics could abate with his strange light.

While the city darkens, he continues to turn each palm
　　　　　skyward, an offering of damp stone,
　　　　a leaf caught in the crack of his right palm. Water

falls from his eyes and behind him, the wind
　　　　　tears a hole in the roof of the church.
　　　　The rain enters the roof, floods

the Holtkamp pipe organ until everything is silent
　　　　　of music. His hands are quieted
　　　　of their pale prayers—the left forefinger

and thumb broken off by a brick spinning its red stream
　　　　　into the air. They push away
　　　　from his body. He watches

the city float past with its shattered glass, shoes,
telephone wire. How the debris of his
broken fingers swirl away from him, then point back.

FRAGMENTS OF AN AFTERMATH

He was laying like he was in a running position—

~

Police need to stick together, Alec Brown testified. *They were
all animals and they deserved to be shot. They were all destroying the city.*

~

She asked him to blink his eyes.

~

We have authority by martial law to shoot looters, one officer
shouted into the rotary-bladed air.

~

Outside a Rite-Aid, a woman on a bicycle
tells a reporter: *I'm a diabetic. I need
test strips, insulin. It hasn't been on ice.*

~

This person, in the car on the levee—

~

A roadway flare was tossed into the car. A gun
was fired into the windshield at the body.

~

*I was kind of thinking if they saw us
on the ground, they wouldn't shoot us.*

~

A black cloud of smoke billowed behind them.
*He looked through the window and could see
that Oakwood Shopping Center was in flames.*

~

Take the city back *and* shoot
to kill *was heard over
the dispatch system more than once.*

～

Inside the scorched sedan: black ashes
and bones. A charred skull, shards of rib.

～

We looted a store because we had no food and we had to do something.

～

If you can sleep with it, do it—

～

Do you support the death penalty for minor thefts?

～

Carrying toothpaste, toothbrushes,
mouthwash, a man stares into
the camera: *All of this is personal
hygiene. I ain't getting nothing
to get drunk or high with.*

～

Do what you have to do.

～

No, the man shouted, *that's everybody's store.*

～

*In a state of occupation, ordinary
citizens are turned into enemies—and corpses.*

～

I forgive these men, said Edna Glover, still holding a picture of her son.

～

At some point, you lost your compass.

～

I've got to get back to my children, she said.
I've got to get back to my children.

FLOOD

for Christopher Lirette

All the balconies were shard-tossed, broken

by the wind. You held your important saves
on the red eye north to Chicago: someone's
Collected Works, a train set with a missing

engine. Your Claiborne Street, your *bon temps*,
grew smaller as the plane climbed

above the delta and paddle boats, the speck

of your roof. A painted orange X,
a sea's swallow. Along the Gulf
where the house of your childhood stood,

each pane bubbled out of its framed socket,
the power lines split

the muddied ground. When you left

the city for what you said was for good,
your voice static and high wind,
you were still flooded, a ditch

filled with debris, a refrigerator

taped shut. Your house
ten feet below the canal's ruined edge.

DOWN IN THE 9

2005

In the shadow of his house, Fats Domino
climbs from broken shards

of an attic window. His body is flashbulb-

stunned, humid. The floorboards
give and splinter behind him, open

to water. Wild

hair, sweat. For days, the city was song-
sodden, newspaper-inked. For days,

he watched the dark

flood rise fifteen feet,
did not know that all over the country

houses burned with the blue

flicker of television, the missing
poster of his face, or how in Ohio,

a radio crooned *Ain't That a Shame.*

Up and down the block, he hears
whistles through fingers, then a boat

under the eaves. Tonight, he breathes

in the heat of himself, this world

of sewage and snakes, the sea-

sick waves, a hand

under the pit of his arm. Tonight,
he steps out into the flashlit dark,

returns himself to the small explosions

of light.

6220 CAMP STREET

The morning of the strange wind,
        I opened tin cans,
scooped chicken livers into pie plates. The city

           emptied of trumpets, neon,
loaves of bread. All around me,

a shotgun of nails. I unpacked boxes
        of tempera, acrylic,
synthetic bristles.
          When the oak fell across the lawn,
        I sat in the hallway and drew

its chalk outline. The city
        became soft, there, dark
water slashed across paper. I counted

           shed claws in the red rug,
      rubbed whiskers with my thumbs.

When the light rose again, its bright splinter
        cracked every surface: broken
window, the street

          a canvas of roof tiles.
        I filled my pockets

with black slate, these chipped
        relics. In my hands, I painted this
ruin into a strip of starlight,

slash of half-moon. For days
there was nothing but oil smears, gloss

of orange, my cat-circled shins. On a napkin,
I watched water turn each greenburst, pop
of blue into shredded leaves, mold-blooms, a buried sky.

PRAYER AT SAINT ROCK CEMETERY

All Souls' Day, 2005

Dear _____, give us peace. We are grieving
in this city of the dead, this world of brick

and plaster. Because most of the flower shops
are still closed, and because nothing

grows here except the smell of mold
and bodies in attics curling into the street,

we miss our crowds of chrysanthemums,
our greenery placed on tombs, and yes,

the plastic wrapping that contains such
tenderness. Dear _____,

clear the rain that covers the broken
paths and graves like a garment,

the sepia stain of floodwater that rings
seven feet high in all directions. At dusk,

we will light small candles, offer what we have:
MREs, crucifixes, photographs

of a still-standing house. We will listen
as the explosions of jackhammers

and wrecking balls dwindle into darkness
while the tombs are scrubbed until each resembles

a new tooth jutting from the earth. Tonight,

we are sentimental for a good meal, a roof,

a bright bouquet. Dear _____,
heal this troubled picture, this city

of static and camera flashes. This
flowerless and crumbled grave.

NEW ORLEANS SNOW GLOBE
2005

Inside the ceramic city, a man

decants a few notes on a sax
under the black and white
Bourbon Street sign. Miniature

tourists eat lemon ices, stir
cream into chicory coffee

in Jackson Square. Because it is Christmas,
wreaths hang from St. Louis Cathedral
and an alligator wearing a Santa suit

waves and waves through the dome's
clear glass. Inside the Dome,

all of the lights are out. Every window

black, empty. Inside the glass,
the dome has gone dry. It is unclear

how much time this takes

or how it happens. It is Christmas here
and the water has released the city—
landlocked the paddleboat, the alligator—

into air, its residue, its white debris.

THE CITY THAT CARE FORGOT

You were here once; you will be here again. —Joanna Klink

What brings you back is the sugared air

that seeps its way through
the streets. The scrolled iron balconies,
banana-leaved courtyards, gas lamps draped

with bright plastic beads. Not the water-

stained drywall, crushed fence, the X-
marked houses. Not the ruin
of mosquito fever, flood, the history

of bodies hung by the neck in trees,
but how the river collects daylight, the sound

of trumpets in late afternoon. You return to this

humid sweep, the second lines of handkerchiefs,
magnolia in every scene. Long ago,
this was the city that care forgot: mold-scarred,

splintered chairs washing upstream. A city
of tents, of wind-wrapped shutters, shotgun

houses. What brings you back. The city

turns its umbrellas in the sun, lights fire
for roux. What calls you: the music

of a gate opening onto Tchoupitoulas Street,
chicory-heat, the roof tiles

in the black sky. The water. The rising.

WHY NEW ORLEANS

for Halli McKee

Because after I left you standing on the balcony
of your apartment, the humidity
entering my body as a whisper might, I knew

the city would follow me back to my own city

of strip malls and bayous, of parking lots
and a neighborhood of noisy children. Because

when I watched you bend to pick up tangles
of bright beads in a potted palm,
watched the afternoon sweep across

a courtyard of banana trees, watched

the feral cats rattle garbage bins as a gate swung
open, then closed, and open again, I loved the ruin

of the cracked porch, the swampy stink of summer
in my hair, the coffee and fried dough, and yes, even
the palmetto bugs that hid just under the window.

Because this was too much to hold—

the dark oaks, the saxophone—
that I had to write it down,

carry it with me. I wanted to remember its flame,
its color of smoke easing out of doorways into the heart
of an alley. I wanted to place its language

on my tongue and taste what was missing.

GRAY LINE KATRINA TOURS

On Decatur Street, a man holds a sign that reads *Gray Line*

Katrina Tours and talks about mold, how he found
his neighbor's roof in his yard after days
of wading through water, the water so deep

he kept spitting out mouthfuls. *It tasted like burnt tires,*

he says, wiping away the summer sweat. A bus fills
with tourists: a man checking film, a woman tying
and untying her hair, each face loaded into a square

of window. Two women ask the tour guide
if there are still bodies in the houses (no)

and what they will be able to see. I am no better at this,

standing in the burnt-sugar sunlight, drinking
chicory coffee from a Styrofoam cup. The brochure
in my hand shows a man wearing a t-shirt that reads

Make Levees Not War, his entire house collapsed

behind him. Another picture shows a concrete slab, another
an aerial view of nothing but water, the dark
storm surged through buildings. Part of me wants to see

the weight of so much disaster: wind-ripped trees,

the cracked teeth of window after window. Part of me
wants to stand in the near-dusk watching a woman snap

a picture of her husband and the guide,

a burst of lightning in the humid haze. Part of me
wants to watch the bus pull into the distance of a coastline

of frail houses and scattered roof tiles, then walk away.

JAZZ FUNERAL

2006

On the street,
once in January
                you were
                carried, your body.

In front of shotgun houses, the bayou.
                In front of storm shutters, magnolia, oleander

leaves, a trumpet's brassed mourn
weaved through umbrellas, parked cars, handkerchiefs.

The yards still spoke of water.

The box, the horse, the carriage,
everything was speaking of water,

then, abandoned windows,
shoes without feet, even

                you. Months before,

I filled entire city blocks. Beds,
the music of thunder. Once
in the after-
                noon, your face was mine.

                The day
you stood in the attic—

you, follicle and fingernail,
even the trumpet

in your hand. All this
      and now. The music

ran you back to the ground.
On the way out, the light-
      hearted, the sound of street-

cars, beads, backtrack. You
should have seen this. Heard

them cut your body
loose. Their knees, feet,
      tapped you away. The children

ran behind. A little boy and his
horn. The drum. The twirl. The debris.

LATE PASTORAL
2010

How beautiful this was in the beginning:
white mulberry, Indian corn, a source

without suffering, without crime.

The blue-white wall of sky above us
                              and nothing for miles but water,
duckweed, Tupelo gum. It is April and the sky

streaks auburn and on the horizon, a fire burns
                              into the sea. It is May, then June,
and August, and heat drifts in from the Gulf

and don't think that we have forgotten
                              what wind can do, how it can peel through

fingers of marshland, rush in its damp color. It is August
and we watch the crime unfold

through eddies and inlets, on each boat
that docks with rings of ochre oil.

        ∼

                        Early evening: a man calls his son
back from the water's edge. The water
                    laps in an egret. They do not touch it,

but see how the dark slick has filled its mouth,
                              covered its eyes. The water
offers the body, then pushes it back

into the brackish dusk. Its chemical smell

fills the mouths of men scraping the sand
with rakes. They watch what washes ashore:

blue crab, wire grass, small balls of dark tar,
          watch the beach dissolve into oil-
coated stalks of Rouseau cane, a net of dead fish.

          ~

          How beautiful this was when the sun flickered
                    silver in its earnest rising. How much we want
to unstrangle the marshes, the oil-rolled shoreline, to return

to the light in the cypress, the mangrove, oxgrass. The stirring
of seabirds rising, rising.

NOTES

The epigraph comes from Italo Calvino's *Invisible Cities*, Harvest Books, 1978.

"Casket Girls": Women brought from France by the Ursuline nuns from 1728–1751 to provide suitable wives for colonists were called "casket girls" due to the shape of their chests of clothing and linens.

"The Good Friday Fire": Within five hours this March 21st fire destroyed 856 of the 1,100 structures in the French Quarter, many of them notable landmarks. The fire was caused by a lit candle.

"Chloe": In 1796, Clark Woodruff caught Chloe, his slave and lover, eavesdropping. As a result, his wife insisted he cut off her ear. Chloe then killed Woodruff's wife and children by lacing a cake with boiled oleander leaves. She was hanged by other slaves.

"Our Lady of Prompt Succor Speaks of Fire": Many people believe that by the intercession of Our Lady of Prompt Succor, the patroness of New Orleans, the Ursuline convent was saved from the Second Great Fire of 1812.

"Report On Levee Breach, 1816": The only way to protect the city from experiencing the devastating effects of a levee breach was by constantly patrolling the levee, often helped by slaves and free Blacks.

"Testimony of Baroness de Pontalba, 1834": Baroness Micaela Almonester de Pontalba was shot four times at point-blank range by her father-in-law, Baron Joseph Delfau de Pontalba, who was enraged at her attempts to divorce his son, Celestin. She survived to go on to commission the famous Pontalba Apartments in Jackson Square.

"Harriet Beecher Stowe at the Cornstalk Hotel, 1850": Harriet Beecher Stowe allegedly stopped at the Cornstalk Hotel in the French Quarter and was inspired to write *Uncle Tom's Cabin* after seeing nearby slave markets.

"American Plague": In 1853, New Orleans suffered its worst epidemic of yellow fever, known as the "American Plague," killing approximately 9,000 people.

"The Disordered Body": According to Ari Kelman in *A River and Its City*, the disproportionate number of Creole and Blacks affected by yellow fever led many wealthy white New Orleanians to believe they were immune, citing the disease preferred "disordered bodies and disordered surroundings."

"Mourning Brooch and Earrings, c. 1866": Mourning jewelry, or hair jewelry, was made by the mourner or by artists using hair clipped from the deceased.

"Sister Xavier's Herb Garden": Sister Francis Xavier Hebert, one of the original Ursuline nuns, was the first pharmacist in Louisiana and the first woman pharmacist in America.

"A Brief History with Documents": On June 7th, 1892, Homer Plessy, who was 1/8th Black, was arrested for entering a whites-only railcar. The incident was orchestrated by attorney Albion Tourgée in order to get the Supreme Court to declare segregation laws unconstitutional.

"Order of the Garter": Between 1895 and 1915, "blue books" were published in Storyville, New Orleans' red-light district. They were guides to the district's services and were inscribed with the motto: *Order of the Garter: Honi Soit Qui Mal Y Pense* (Shame to Him Who Evil Thinks).

"Photograph of Hilma Burt's Mirrored Ballroom with Jelly Roll Morton, 1907": Famed musician, Jelly Roll Morton, got his start playing the piano in the ballroom of a brothel in Storyville.

"Mayann": Mayann Albert, the mother of jazz legend Louis Armstrong, made her living as a prostitute. For many years, she abandoned Armstrong, who was raised by his grandmother.

"The Good Friday Flood, 1927": Fifteen inches of rain within 18 hours caused water to rise four feet. The city's banking committee and Dock Board decided to dynamite a levee, resulting in the displacement of thousands of residents, most of whom were never compensated for their losses.

"Testimony of Evangeline the Oyster Girl, 1948": A burlesque dancer by the name of Evangeline Sylvas (Kitty West) was featured in *LIFE* magazine for ruining a rival dancer's act on stage and then being put in jail.

"The Heel String Gang": In 1952, 31 inmates of Angola Prison, considered the worst prison in America, cut their Achilles' tendons to protest the hard work and brutality.

"The Education of Ruby Bridges, 1960": On November 14, 6-year-old Ruby Bridges was the first Black student to enroll at William Frantz Public Elementary School. Her presence set off protests and an exodus of white students from the school and schools throughout the city.

"Billion-Dollar Betsy": Hurricane Betsy caused surge waters to rise 10 feet in some areas and levee breaches to flood parts of Gentilly, the Upper Ninth Ward, and the Lower Ninth Ward, devastating 164,000 homes. Betsy was the first hurricane to cause damage in excess of $1 billion.

"Highway Pastoral": In 1966, construction began on the elevated leg of the I-10 extension on North Claiborne Avenue as part of the 1956 Federal Aid Highway Act. The construction claimed more than 500 homes and businesses, and 70 percent of the trees in the historic Treme district, which had until that time been one of the oldest racially diverse neighborhoods in the United States.

"The Chicken Man Walks the Quarter": Fred Staten was a New Orleans nightclub performer and also considered by locals as the King of Voodoo.

"The Stella/Stanley Shouting Contest": Each year the Tennessee Williams Literary Festival hosts the Stella/Stanley Shouting Contest in which entrants call "Stella!" (or "Stanley!") three times and are judged on loudness and emotion.

"The Wishing Tomb": In St. Louis Cemetery No. 2, the great Voodoo Queen Marie Laveau's vault is distinguished as "the wishing tomb." Young women petition her there when seeking husbands.

"Wind Prayer": According to *Gumbo Tales* by Sarah Roahen, "Devout and superstitious New Orleanians store broken pieces of blessed bread in freezers leftover from St. Joseph's Day, until hurricane season at which time they throw the bread into the wind as an active prayer for bad weather to abate."

"Fragments of an Aftermath": Four days after Hurricane Katrina, Henry Glover, a 31-year-old Black man was found shot and burned to death in a car parked on a Mississippi River levee. Officer David Warren, who was convicted of the shooting, believed Glover was looting a local store. The language in this poem draws from the following articles and is indebted to those who shared their stories: "After Katrina, Cops Given OK to Shoot Looters," CBS News, August 30, 2010; "Looters and the lessons of Katrina," *Los Angeles Times*, August 29, 2010; "Looters take advantage of New Orleans mess," MSNBC, August 30, 2005; "In a city without rules, is looting OK?" MSNBC, September 5, 2005; "Officer fired at unarmed, fleeing man, his partner tells federal jury in Henry Glover case," *The Times-Picayune*, November 10, 2010; "Two former NOPD officers receive stiff sentences in Henry Glover case," *The Times-Picayune*, March 31, 2011; and "Where are the Japanese looters?" *Washington Times*, March 14, 2011.

"6220 Camp Street": Artist Ellen Montgomery, 85, lived with 33 cats, and refused to evacuate during Katrina because she did not want to abandon them.

"The City That Care Forgot": The epigraph comes from the poem, "Winter Field," in Joanna Klink's book *Circadian*, Penguin (Non-Classics), 2007.

ACKNOWLEDGEMENTS

Grateful acknowledgement is made to the following journals and anthologies where these poems appeared, some in slightly different versions:

5AM: "Washer Woman, 1917"

The Allegheny Review: "Billion-Dollar Betsy"

Anti-: "Decorating the Tombs: All Saints' Day," "Holt Cemetery"

Bellevue Literary Review: "The Disordered Body"

Crab Creek Review: "The Angola Inmate Coffin Factory," "Why New Orleans"

Crab Orchard Review: "American Plague"

diode: "6220 Camp Street," "The Wishing Tomb"

Gigantic Sequins: "The Chicken Man Walks the Quarter"

The Greensboro Review: "Mourning Brooch with Hair and Earrings, c. 1866"

The Journal: "Casket Girls," "The Good Friday Flood, 1927"

Linebreak: "Early Pastoral," "Photograph of Hilma Burt's Mirrored Ballroom with Jelly Roll Morton, 1907"

The Nepotist: "Flood"

North American Review: "The City That Care Forgot"

The Offending Adam: "Do You Know What It Means," "Harriet Beecher Stowe at the Cornstalk Hotel, 1850," "Testimony of Baroness de Pontalba," "The City That Care Forgot"

Indiana Review: "Mayann"

Superstition Review: "Brief History with Documents," "Down in the 9," "Jazz Funeral"

Zone 3: "Marie Laveau," "The Heel String Gang"

The poem "Love Spell with Hair and Oil" appeared in *Two Weeks Anthology: A Digital Anthology of Contemporary Poetry* (*Linebreak*, 2011), edited by Ash Bowen and Johnathon Williams.

Special thanks are offered to the following: Barbara Auchter, Julie Bloemeke, Blas Falconer, Katie Ford, Eddie Gonzalez, Chris Lirette, Nathan McClain, Jo Ellen Porter, Eddy Roberts, Leslie Contreras Schwartz, Matthew Siegel, Marissa Sinisi, Patricia Smith, Rebecca Wadlinger, and Jeffrey Wood.

I am especially grateful to Susan Kan for the guidance, suggestions, and attention given to this book.

ABOUT THE AUTHOR

Amanda Auchter is the founding editor of *Pebble Lake Review*, and the author of *The Glass Crib*, winner of the 2010 Zone 3 Press First Book Award, and the chapbook, *Light Under Skin*. She has received numerous awards and honors including the Theodore Morrison Poetry Scholarship from the Bread Loaf Writers' Conference, the Marica and Jan Vilcek Prize for Poetry, the Mary C. Mohr Poetry Award, and the James Wright Poetry Award. She holds an MFA from the Bennington Writing Seminars and teaches creative writing and literature at Lone Star College in Houston, Texas.

ABOUT PERUGIA PRESS

Perugia Press publishes one collection of poetry each year, by a woman at the beginning of her publishing career. Our mission is to produce beautiful books that interest long-time readers of poetry and welcome those new to poetry. We also aim to celebrate and promote poetry whenever we can, and to keep the cultural discussion of poetry inclusive.

Also from Perugia Press:
- *Gloss,* Ida Stewart
- *Each Crumbling House,* Melody S. Gee
- *How to Live on Bread and Music,* Jennifer K. Sweeney
- *Two Minutes of Light,* Nancy K. Pearson
- *Beg No Pardon,* Lynne Thompson
- *Lamb,* Frannie Lindsay
- *The Disappearing Letters,* Carol Edelstein
- *Kettle Bottom,* Diane Gilliam Fisher
- *Seamless,* Linda Tomol Pennisi
- *Red,* Melanie Braverman
- *A Wound On Stone,* Faye George
- *The Work of Hands,* Catherine Anderson
- *Reach,* Janet E. Aalfs
- *Impulse to Fly,* Almitra David
- *Finding the Bear,* Gail Thomas

This book was typeset in Arno Pro, a type family designed in 2007 by Robert Slimbach for Adobe Systems, Inc.

The type, both beautiful and legible, combines classical letterforms with a warm and graceful calligraphic style.